CROCE'S PHILOSOPHY OF HISTORY

CROCE'S PHILOSOPHY OF HISTORY

BY

R. G. COLLINGWOOD

KALPAZ

ISBN: 978-93-5128-789-6(HB)

First Published in 1921
Indian Reprint in 2017

Published by

Kalpaz Publications
C-30, Satyawati Nagar,
Delhi – 110052
E-mail: kalpaz@hotmail.com
Website: kalpazpublications.com
Ph.: +91-9212142040

Cataloging in Publication Data—DK
Courtesy: D.K. Agencies (P) Ltd. <docinfo@dkagencies.com>

Collingwood, R. G. (Robin George), 1889-1943, **author.**
Croce's philosophy of history / by R.G. Collingwood.
pages cm
"First published in 1921"—Title page verso.
ISBN 9789351287896

1. Croce, Benedetto, 1866-1952. 2. History—Philosophy. I. Title.

D16.8.C65 2017 DDC 901 23

CROCE'S PHILOSOPHY OF HISTORY.

R. G. COLLINGWOOD,

Fellow of Pembroke College, Oxford.

AN alliance between philosophy and history is no new idea in this country. Most Englishmen who know or care anything about philosophy have been influenced, directly or indirectly, by the "Greats" school at Oxford; and the distinguishing mark of this school is the connection which it maintains between the study of ancient history and that of ancient philosophy. It is this connection that gives Oxford philosophy its chief merit, a fine tradition of scholarship and interpretation in Plato and Aristotle; and it is, perhaps, the failure to extend the same principle to the study of more recent thought that has led in this school to a much lower standard in the interpretation of modern philosophy, unsupported as it is by any study of modern history.

The ideal of a combined study of philosophy and history is energetically supported by Croce. Himself a philosopher of eminence and an accomplished historian, he feels acutely in his own person the profit which each of his pursuits in turn derives from the other. The historian must study the philosophy of his period if he is to understand those forces which ultimately shaped its destiny; if he does not follow the thoughts of the men whose actions he is studying he can never enter into the life of his period, and can at best observe it from outside as a sequence of unexplained facts, or facts to be explained by physical causes alone. And the philosopher must in his turn study history. How else is he to understand why certain problems at certain times pressed for solution on the philosopher's mind? How else is he to understand the individual philosopher's temperament, his outlook on life, the very symbolism and language in which he has expressed himself? In short, if the philosopher is to understand the

history of philosophy he must study the general history of humanity; and a philosophy which ignores its own history is a philosophy which spends its labour only to rediscover errors long dead.

History without philosophy is history seen from the outside, the play of mechanical and unchanging forces in a materialistically conceived world: philosophy without history is philosophy seen from the outside, the veering and backing, rising and falling, of motiveless winds of doctrine. "Both these are monsters." But history fertilised by philosophy is the history of the human spirit in its secular attempt to build itself a world of laws and institutions in which it can live as it wishes to live; and philosophy fertilised by history is the progressive raising and solving of the endless intellectual problems whose succession forms the inner side of this secular struggle. Thus the two studies which, apart, degenerate into strings of empty dates and lists of pedantic distinctions—"To seventeen add two, And Queen Anne you will view," "Barbara celarent darii ferioque prioris"—become, together, a single science of all things human.

This is the point of view from which Croce proposes, and in his own work carries out, a closer union between philosophy and history. It is a point of view which must interest English readers; the more so as in these days, when the pre-eminence of classical studies in English education is a thing of the past, the position of philosophy as a subject of study demands the closest attention. In the past the Oxford "Greats" school has stood for this ideal of the cross-fertilisation of history and philosophy, even when the co-ordination of the two sides has been worst, and the undergraduate has seemed to be merely reading two different schools at once, under tutors who regarded each other as rivals for his attention; but in the future the whole question will be reopened, and philosophy may either contract a new alliance with the natural sciences, or retire into single blessedness as an independent subject of study like Forestry or Geography, or force herself into the company of Modern History, disguised perhaps under the inoffensive name of Political Theory. To solve this problem in the best way it is necessary to have a clear idea of what philosophy is, and what are its relations to these other subjects of study. These, of course, are controversial questions, on which no one can lay down the law; but the conclusions of Croce demand at least our attention, and we propose here to discuss his views on the nature of history and its relation to philosophy. As our purpose is rather to criticise than to

expound, we shall select some of his views and examine these as typical of the whole.

The book in which he expounds them is the *Teoria e Storia della Storiografia* (Bari, 1917), which, like many of Croce's books, falls into two sections, a theoretical and a historical. The relation between the two is close; the ideas which are discussed in the former are exemplified in the latter, and the process of development followed in the latter is only intelligible in the light of the principles laid down in the former. Our concern here is especially with the theoretical section; not because it is the most striking—the historical section is a rapid but extremely brilliant survey of the progress of historical thought, in which the characteristics of succeeding periods are set forth with a penetration and fairness which could hardly be bettered—but because our present business is the explicit statement of theoretical principles.

In order to arrive at a clear concept of what history is, Croce begins by telling us what it is not. It is not annals. That is to say, it is not the lists of dates with which a superficial observer confuses it. To the outward eye, a book may consist of mere chronological tables; but to the historian these tables mean real history, not because they are, but because they stand for, the thought which is history. History goes on in the mind of the historian: he thinks it, he enacts it within himself: he identifies himself with the history he is studying and actually lives it as he thinks it, whence Croce's paradox that "all history is contemporary history." Annals, on the other hand, belong to the past; the schoolboy learning a list of dates does not live them in his thought, but takes them as something alien imposed upon him from outside—brute facts, dead and dry; no living reality such as his teacher, if he is a good historian, can enjoy in reading the same list. Annals, then, are past history, and therefore not history at all. They are the dry bones of history, its dead corpse.

This is illuminating, and satisfactory enough until we begin to reflect upon it. History is thought, annals the corpse of thought. But has thought a corpse? and if so, what is it like? The corpse of a organism is something other than the organism itself: what, for an idealistic philosopher like Croce, is there other than thought, in terms of which we can give a philosophically satisfactory definition of the corpse of thought?

Croce's general "philosophy of the spirit" supples him with a ready-made answer. Nothing exists but the spirit; but the spirit has two sides or parts, thought and will. Whatever is not thought is will. If you find some fact which cannot

be explained as an instance of thought, you must explain it as an instance of will. Thought is the synthesis of subject and object, and its characteristic is truth: will is the creation of an object by the subject, and its characteristic is utility. Wherever you find something which appears at first sight to be an example of thinking, but which on inspection is found not to possess the quality of truth, it follows that it must be an example of willing, and possess the quality of usefulness. Such, in a rough outline, is the principle of analysis which Croce applies in this book and elsewhere. History is thought: there is here a perfect synthesis of subject and object, inasmuch as the historian thinks himself into the history, and the two become contemporary. Annals are not thought but willed; they are constructed—"drawn up"—by the historian for his own ends; they are a convention serving the purposes of historical thought, as musical notation serves the purposes of musical thought without being musical thought; they are not true but useful.

This is the answer which Croce gives, or rather tries to give, to the question we raised. But he does not really succeed in giving it. He cannot bring himself to say that annals are simply devoid of truth, are in no sense an act of thought. That would amount to saying that annals are the words, and history their meaning: which would not be what he wanted. So he says that annals are (p. 9) "sounds, or graphic symbols representing sounds, held together and maintained not by an act of thought which thinks them (in which case they would once more be supplied with content), but by an act of will which thinks it useful for certain purposes of its own to preserve these words, empty or half empty though they be." "Or half empty." This is a strange reservation. Are the words of which annals are composed, then, not empty after all? Are they half full, half full, that is, of thought? But if so, the distinction between the act of thought and the act of will has broken down: annals are only history whose words mean less indeed than the same words as used by history proper, but still have meaning, are still essentially vehicles of thought. And Croce would be the first to admit and insist that a difference of degree has nothing to do with a philosophical question like this.

This is not the only passage in which Croce's clearness of vision and common sense break through the abstractions of his formal philosophy. He tries to maintain a philosophy according to which every act of the spirit falls under either one or the other of two mutually exclusive heads (theoretical

and practical), subdivided into four sub-heads (intuition and thought; economic willing and ethical willing), so related that the second and fourth sub-heads involve the first and third respectively (thought is also intuition, ethical action is also economic action), but not *vice versa*. Now this formal philosophy of the mind is purely psychological and empirical in character; it is what Croce himself calls "naturalism" or "transcendence." And with that side of himself which never ceases to combat all kinds of naturalism, he combats this philosophy of his own with the rest. To go into this fully would involve a detailed analysis of Croce's other works, and we shall not pursue it here. But we must refer to it, and insist upon this general principle: that there are two Croces, the realist, dualist, empiricist, or naturalist, who delights in formal distinctions and habitually works in dualistic or transcendent terms, and the idealist, whose whole life is a warfare upon transcendence and naturalism in all their forms, who sweeps away dualisms and reunites distinctions in a concrete or immanent unity. A great part of Croce's written work consists in a debate between these two, one building up dualisms and the other dismantling them; sometimes failing to dismantle them. This we shall find throughout the present book. In fact, at the end of our inquiry, we shall see reason to suspect that this double-mindedness has now become so intolerable to Croce himself that he feels impelled to destroy altogether a philosophy so deeply at variance with itself, and to take refuge in a new field of activity.

The dualism between history and annals is really, if I understand it aright, an expository or "pedagogic" dualism, confused by the attempt to interpret it as a real or philosophical dualism, to which end it has been mistakenly identified with the distinction between a symbol and its meaning. An expository dualism is a common enough device: in order to expound a new idea one frequently distinguishes it point by point from an old, thereby developing what looks like a dualism between them, without, however, at all meaning to imply that the dualism is real, and that the old conception has a permanent place in one's philosophy alongside of the new. Thus the antithesis between the flesh and the spirit, developed in order to define the term spirit, is misunderstood if it is hardened into a metaphysical dualism: so again that between mind and matter, art and nature, and so forth. In such cases the two terms are not names for two co-ordinate realities, but an old and a new name for the same thing, or even an old and a new "definition of the Absolute," and the new supersedes

the old: if the old is compelled to live on alongside the new, it sets up a dualism whose effect is precisely to destroy the whole meaning of the new conception and to characterise the whole view as a naturalistic or transcendent philosophy.

This is curiously illustrated by Croce's chapter on "History and Annals." "History is living history, annals are dead history: history is contemporary history, annals are past history: history is primarily an act of thought, annals an act of will" (p. 10). Here again the word *primarily* gives everything away; but, ignoring that, it is strange that the category in which annals fall is indifferently, and as it were synonymously, called *the past*, *dead*, and *the will*. Here—and numerous other passages could be quoted which prove the same thing—Croce is really identifying the distinction of thought and will with the distinction of living and dead, spirit and matter. The will is thought of as the non-spiritual: that is to say, the concept of dead matter has reappeared in the heart of idealism, christened by the strange name of will. This name is given to it because, while Croce holds the idealistic theory that thought thinks itself, he unconsciously holds the realistic or transcendent theory that the will wills not itself but the existence of a lifeless object other than itself, something unspiritual held in existence by an act of the will. Thus, wherever Croce appeals from the concept of thought to the concept of will, he is laying aside his idealism and falling back into a transcendent naturalism.

But now the idealist reasserts himself. A corpse, after all, is not merely dead: it is the source of new life. So annals are a necessary part of the growth of history: thought, as a philosopher has said, "feeds saprophytically upon its own corpse." Annals are therefore not a mere stupid perversion of history, but are essential to history itself. Annals are a "moment" of history, and so therefore is will of thought, matter of mind, death of life, error of truth. Error is the negative moment of thought, without which the positive or constructive moment, criticism, would have nothing to work upon. Criticism in destroying error constructs truth. So historical criticism, in absorbing and digesting annals, in showing that they are not history, creates the thought that is history. This is idealism; but it stultifies the original dualism. The distinction between history and annals is now not a distinction between what history is (thought) and what history is not (will), but between one act of thought (history) and another act of thought of the same kind, now superseded and laid aside (annals), between the half-truth of an earlier stage

in the process of thought and the fuller truth that succeeds it. This is no dualism, no relation between A and not-A, and therefore it cannot be symbolised by the naturalistic terminology of thought and will; it is the dialectical relation between two phases of one and the same development, which is throughout a process of both thinking and willing.

The same fundamental vice underlies the very attractive discussion of "pseudo-histories." We all know the historian who mistakes mere accuracy for truth, the "philological" historian; and him who mistakes romance for history, the "poetical" historian; and him who imagines that the aim of history is not to tell the truth but to edify or glorify or instruct, the "pragmatic" historian. And Croce characterises them and discusses their faults in an altogether admirable way. But he wants to prove that he has given us a list of all the possible forms of false history, and this can be done by appealing to the list of the "forms of the spirit." But the appeal not only fails in detail—for his list of pseudo-histories tallies very ill with the list of forms of the spirit—but is false in principle.

For "poetical" history, to take an example, is only a name calling attention to a necessary feature of all history. Croce shows how Herodotus, Livy, Tacitus, Grote, Mommsen, Thierry, and so forth, all wrote from a subjective point of view, wrote so that their personal ideals and feelings coloured their whole work and in parts falsified it. Now, if this is so, who wrote real history, history not coloured by points of view and ideals? Clearly, no one. It is not even desirable that anyone should. History, to be, must be seen, and must be seen by somebody, from somebody's point of view. And doubtless, every history so seen will be in part seen falsely. But this is not an accusation against any particular school of historians; it is a law of our nature. The only safe way of avoiding error is to give up looking for the truth.

And here, curiously, Croce breaks out into a panegyric on error, as if conscious that he was being too hard on it. The passage is a most interesting combination of naturalism and idealism. Error, says Croce, is not a "fact"; it is a "spirit"; it is "not a Caliban, but an Ariel, breathing, calling, and enticing from every side, and never by any effort to be solidified into hard fact." This image implies that error does not, as such, exist; that is, that no judgment is wholly or simply erroneous, wholly devoid of truth: which is orthodox idealism, but quite contrary to Croce's general theory of error. But it also implies that error as such is valuable and good: he speaks

definitely of the "salutary efficacy of error"; and this conflicts not only with the description of pseudo-histories as "pathological"—and therefore, presumably, to be wholly avoided—but also with Croce's own idealism, and with the view which surely seems reasonable, that the indubitable value and efficacy of errors belongs to them not *qua* errors but *qua* (at least partial) truths. An error like historical materialism is, as Croce says, not a fact; that is because, its falsity discovered, it is banished, it becomes a memory. Also, as Croce says, it is, or rather we should say was, useful: it superseded a worse error, historical romanticism. But it was once a fact, and then it was a truth—the best truth that could be had then, anyhow; and then, too, it was useful, as an improvement on its predecessor. To-day it is not a fact (except for historians of thought), nor true, nor yet useful. The passage is confused because Croce is assigning to error as such the merits of truth; which is an attempt to express the fact that error as such does not exist, and that what we call an error is in part true and therefore has the "salutary efficacy" which belongs to truth alone. This confusion is due to the vacillation between naturalism, for which some statements are just true and others just false, and idealism, for which truth and falsehood are inextricably united in every judgment, in so far as it creates itself by criticising another, and becomes itself in turn the object of further criticism.

This vacillation is the more interesting as much of Croce's treatment of error is purely naturalistic, and shows no trace of idealism. His general theory of error, in the *Logica*, is absolutely naturalistic. Thought, he there argues, is as such true, and can never be erroneous: an error, whatever it is, cannot be a thought. What is it, then? Why, an act of will. We need hardly point out the absurdities of such a theory. We only wish to point out its naturalistic character; to lay stress on the distinction implied between a truth, as containing no error, and an error, as containing no truth, correlative with that between pure thinking and pure willing, and based on the same naturalistic or transcendent logic. So again his inquiry into the varieties (phenomenology) of error, in this book and elsewhere, and the list of pseudo-histories, are purely naturalistic; and so again is a highly "transcendent" type of argument not uncommon with him, which traces the origin of a philosophical error to the baneful influence of some other activity of the spirit. Thus philosophical errors, which by their very nature can only have arisen within philosophy itself, are ascribed to science (p. 45, the fallacy of the independent object)

and religion (p. 51, the dualism of *a priori* and *a posteriori* truths), errors whose only connection with science or religion is that when philosophers believed in them they applied them to the interpretation of these activities: whereupon Croce, having rejected them as general philosophical principles, uncritically retains them as adequate accounts of activities to which he has not paid special attention, and thus credits these activities with originating them. The result is a kind of mythology, in which Philosophy or Thought takes the part of a blameless and innocent heroine led into errors by the villains Science and Religion. These flights of pure naturalism in Croce have a curious eighteenth-century flavour; it is difficult in reading them to feel ourselves in the forefront of modern philosophy; for Science and Religion, the villains of the piece, represent precisely that Caliban of embodied factual error whose banishment from philosophy has just been ratified by Croce himself.

The same naturalism colours the chapter on the "Positivity of History." Here the doctrine is expounded that "history always justifies, never condemns." History always expresses positive judgments, never negative; that is, it explains why things happened as they did, and this is to prove that they happened rightly. "A fact which seems merely bad is a non-historical fact," a fact not yet thought out successfully by the historian, not yet understood. The historian as such therefore always justifies: if he condemns, he proves himself no historian. What is he, then? Why, a partisan; one who acts instead of thinking, serves practical instead of theoretical needs. The historian as such is a thinker; "the history which once was lived is by him thought, and in thought the antitheses which arose in volition or feeling no longer exist." To condemn in thought is to "confuse thought with life."

Here as usual we sympathise warmly: we know the historian who regards history as a melodrama, and we do not regard him as the best kind of historian. But we are trying at present to think philosophically; and the dualism between thought and life makes us a little uncomfortable. Life, we are told, is the scene of value-judgments, judgments of good and evil, which are products of the will; thought knows only the truth, and in the eye of thought everything that is, is justified. Partiality is proper and necessary to action, impartiality to thought. The statesman calls his opponent wicked or misguided, because, being a man of action and not a man of thought, it is not his business to understand him, but only to defeat him; the historian, understanding the motives of both, calls both alike wise and good.

This is the same tangled skein of idealism and naturalism. The underlying truth, that no historical event, no act and no person, is merely evil, and that it is the duty of the historian to discover and express the good which our hastier analysis of the facts has failed to reveal—this is an important doctrine, and it is an idealistic one; but the terms in which Croce has stated it are naturalistic. The distinction between theoretical and practical men, activities, or points of view is pure naturalism, and here it leads Croce into plain and obvious misstatements. It is monstrous to say that partiality is right and necessary in a statesman and wrong in a historian. Each alike ought to be as impartial as he possibly can in the process of balancing claims and forming a judgment on them; and each must be partial in asserting his judgment, when he has formed it, against his opponent's. The statesman ought to show all the impartiality he can in judging the claims of capital and labour, or agriculture and industry, however energetically he supports his own bills and denounces those of his opponents; and if the historian is impartial in balancing evidence and understanding motives, we do not expect him to be so impartial as to declare a rival's view of the character of Richard III. as good as his own. Because thought must be impartial, are there to be no more controversies?

Controversies, yes, it may be said, but not condemnations. We may refute Mommsen, but we must not condemn Julius Cæsar. But this is quite unreasonable. If I may think a German professor wrong, why not a Roman general? If, as a historian of warfare, I must accept all Cæsar's battles as impeccable, then as a historian of the history of warfare I must accept all Mommsen's accounts of them as impeccable for the same reason. Controversy is for contemporaries, no doubt: *de mortuis nil nisi bonum.* But as Cæsar's historian I am—is not Croce forgetting it?—Cæsar's contemporary. When a man is dead, the world has judged him, and my judgment does not matter; but the mere fact that I am rethinking his history proves that he is not dead, that the world has not yet passed its judgment. In my person, indeed, it is now about to pass judgment. Croce's contention is that I am forbidden to pass any but an exclusively favourable judgment. Why is this? It is because Croce is here assuming a "transcendent" theory of knowledge, according to which judgment has already been passed in a court outside the mind of the historian, a court from which he has no appeal. He can only write down what he finds written on the page of History.

Thus the idealistic principle that there is a positive side in

every historical fact is combined with the naturalistic assumption that the positive side excludes a negative side; the principle that nothing is merely bad is misunderstood as implying that everything is wholly good, and not bad in any sense at all. And this naturalistic misinterpretation of an idealistic principle confuses the whole argument to such an extent that it actually necessitates a naturalistic and transcendent theory of knowledge. Only in the light of such a theory can it be maintained, as Croce here maintains, that every historical event is right, and therefore everyone who thinks otherwise is wrong, as if the opinions of these poor creatures were not also historical events.

The dualism of thought and life is thus pure transcendence, a formal contradiction of Croce's own theory of history. Thought is life, and therefore the historian can never be impartial; he can only struggle to overcome one prejudice after another, and trust to his successors to carry on the work. The progress of thought is always negative in that it means a continual controversy with oneself and within oneself. The abstract "positivity of history" is a delusion, bred of a naturalistic philosophy.

In the same spirit Croce proceeds to expound his conception of progress. There being no negativity in history, that is to say, none in the world of reality, all is progress, every change is, as he says, "a change from the good to the better." There is no such thing as decadence; what appears to be so is really progress, if only you look at it from the right point of view. True; there always is such a point of view, and it is of the utmost importance that we should not overlook it. But there is the opposite point of view too. A change that is really a progress seen from one end is no less really a decadence, seen from the other. It is true to say that the decay of archery was the rise of firearms; but it is not less true to say that the rise of firearms was the decay of archery. Here is one point of view against another: which is the right one? Croce answers emphatically that one is altogether right and the other altogether wrong. But why? Is it the historian's duty always to take the side of the big battalions just because they win? Is he always to side with the gods against Cato? Or do we not rather feel that it was just by siding against Cato that the gods proved themselves no true gods? The historian's duty is surely not to pick and choose: he must make every point of view his own, and not condemn the lost cause merely because it is lost. The fact is that Croce is here again taking a transcendent attitude, asserting the existence of a criterion

outside the historian's mind by which the points of view which arise within that mind are justified and condemned.

It is the less surprising to find this transcendence emerge into full daylight at the end of the chapter. Croce is saying that when a historian fails to maintain a properly "positive" attitude, fails, that is, to maintain that whatever happens is right, he does so because he has attached himself so blindly to a cause, a person, an institution, a truth, as to forget that every individual thing is but mortal; and when his foolish hopes are shattered and the beloved object dies in his arms, the face of the world is darkened and he can see nothing in the change but the destruction of that which he loved, and can only repeat the sad story of its death. "All histories which tell of the decay and death of peoples and institutions are false"; "elegiac history" is always partisan history. This he expands by saying that immortality is the prerogative of the spirit in general: the spirit in its determinate and particular forms always perishes and always must perish.

Here the transcendence is explicit and unequivocal. The "spirit in general" is presented as having characters (immortality, absoluteness) which the individual spirit has not; the whole is the negation of the part; the absolute or infinite is something over against, contrasted with, the finite. The Christianity at which Croce never ceases to gird for its transcendence is here, as often, immanent exactly where he is himself transcendent. It knows that life is reached through death and found in death, and that to live without dying is to die indeed.

The whole discussion of the "positivity of history" is, in fact, vitiated by naturalism. The truth which Croce wishes to express is the same which Hegel concealed beneath his famous phrase, "the real is the rational." What happens, happens for a good reason, and it is the business of history to trace the reason and state it. And that means to justify the event. But this truth is grossly distorted if it is twisted into the service of a vulgar optimism which takes it for the whole truth. Hegel's view of reality, as Croce himself has insisted, was no such vulgar optimism, but a tragic view; and yet the common charge of optimism brought against him is not unfounded, for he, like Croce, had in him a streak of naturalism which at last overcame him. The point of view here maintained by Croce, from which every change is for the better, and all partisans of lost causes are fools and blasphemers, is neither better nor worse in itself than that from which all change is for the worse, and all innovators are Bolsheviks and

scoundrels. A history which was merely a tragedy or a series of tragedies, like the "Monk's Tale" in Chaucer, would be a misrepresentation of reality; but to hold that all tragedy is delusion and error, and that reality contains no tragic elements at all, is to misrepresent it not less gravely. To imagine that the choice lies between these two misrepresentations, that a positive and a negative moment cannot coexist in reality, is just the kind of error that characterises a transcendent or naturalistic philosophy.

We are now in a position to consider the relation between history, science, and philosophy. Science Croce identifies with the generalising activity of the mind. History is the internal and individual understanding of an object into which the mind so enters that subject and object can no longer be separated; it is real thinking. Science is the external and arbitrary construction of abstract types, and the manipulation of them for practical ends; it is not thinking at all, but willing. This is Croce's distinction. It falls, we observe, within the competence of Croce the naturalist, appealing as it does to the abstract scheme of thought and will. What does Croce the idealist say to it? For it is evident that he cannot assent to it.

He answers the question tacitly in a chapter on "Natural History." Here he denounces that kind of "history" which proceeds by making abstract classifications and then spreads out the classes over a chronological scale; for instance, that kind of history of language which imagines that language began by being monosyllabic, and then went on to polysyllabic forms, or that history of morals and society which begins with pure egoism and goes on to "deduce" altruism, and so on. He shows that this type of fallacy, in which temporal sequence is used as a kind of mythology for logical or spacial interrelation, is found not only in the sciences of nature but also in the sciences of man. In both alike, he says, we classify and arrange our facts, and make abstract generalisations which can, if we like, be arranged along an imaginary time-scale. But also, in both alike we can do real thinking: we can enter into the individual and understand it from within. The object, whether "a neolithic Ligurian or a blade of grass," can be penetrated by thought and lived by the thinker.

This simply destroys the distinction between science and history. It proves that as science (abstract classification) enters into the work of the historian, so history (concrete individual thought) enters into the work of the scientist. We are generally told that the business of the scientist consists of

classifying and abstracting: this, we now see, is not the case. A scientist is intrinsically no more concerned with generalising than a historian. Each does generalise; the geologist generalises about classes of rocks, as the historian generalises about classes of manuscripts; but in each case the generalisation is the means to that thinking which is the man's real work. The historian's real work is the reconstruction in thought of a particular historical event; the geologist's, the reconstruction in thought of a particular geological epoch at a particular place. If the anthropologist's aim is to be a neolithic Ligurian, the botanist's is to be a blade of grass.

Croce does not say this explicitly, but it is all implied in what he does say. He is in the habit of maintaining, formally, the naturalistic distinction of science and history, as concerned with generalisations and individuals respectively; but what he calls science is only one fragment of what he knows history to be, and equally it is only one fragment of what science really is. But, not being perhaps so deeply versed in science as he is in history, he readily misunderstands the true nature of scientific thinking, uncritically swallowing whole the naturalistic logic and mistaking one subordinate aspect of science for the whole.

The relation of philosophy to history is a subject often touched on in this book, but in the end left extremely obscure. The obscurity is due to a vacillation between two views; the idealistic strain of Croce's thought maintaining (with Gentile, to whom this side of Croce seems to be not a little indebted) the identity of philosophy and history, and the naturalistic maintaining that philosophy is a component part of history.

The two views are held side by side, without any attempt at reconciliation: probably without consciousness of the discrepancy. But no one who collects the relevant passages can fail to be struck by the contrast. Thus, on p. 17 "philology" (*i.e.* fact) "combines with philosophy" (*i.e.* critical thought) "to form history"; on p. 71 "philosophy is history and history is philosophy"; on p. 186 philosophy is "the methodological moment of history"; and on p. 162 "there is no way of distinguishing historical thought from philosophical." The two views seem to alternate with curious regularity.

The view that history and philosophy are identical is derived from reflections like those with which this paper began. Each without the other is a lifeless corpse: every piece of real thinking is both at once. This is Gentile's view. But the view that philosophy is a mere subordinate moment in history has quite different motives. It seems to indicate

that historical thought is conceived as real or absolute thought, containing philosophy complete within itself; while philosophy by itself is an inferior form, abstract and at best only half true, which requires to be supplemented by "philology" or the study of fact, and so converted into the perfect form of history. We are reminded of Vico's alliance between philosophy and philology by the language here, and of Hegel's dialectic by the thought that one form of activity is inherently imperfect and requires to be transformed into another before it can be satisfactory.

It is to this latter view that Croce seems finally to incline. In an appendix written some years after the body of the book he states it definitely: philosophy is the "methodological moment of history," that is, the working-out and critical construction of the concepts which history employs in its work. And this is an immanent methodology—it goes on not outside history, in a separate laboratory, but within the process of historical thinking itself. The philosopher and the historian have returned from the ride, in fact, with the philosopher inside.

This seems to me to indicate two things: the triumph within philosophy of Croce the naturalist over Croce the idealist, and the shifting of Croce's own centre of interest from philosophy to history.

The naturalist triumphs over the idealist because the synthesis of philosophy and philology in history implies the naturalistic conception of philosophy and philology as two different and antithetical forms of activity, which again implies that ideas or categories, or whatever is the subject-matter of philosophy, are something different from facts, the subject-matter of philology. Such a dualism of idea and fact is wholly impossible to an idealist; and yet only on this assumption can it be maintained that philosophy is immanent in history while history is transcendent with reference to philosophy. Naturalism, transcendence, is the last word.

Further, Croce here shows, if I read his meaning aright, that he is gradually deserting philosophy for history. He appears to have come to the conclusion that philosophical truth is to be attained not by direct fire—by the study of philosophy in the ordinary sense, which he now pronounces a delusion—but indirectly, as a product of ordinary historical work. Philosophy in his mind is being absorbed in history; the two are not poised in equilibrium, as with Gentile, but one is cancelled out entirely as already provided for by the other. This is made clear by the appendix on "Philosophy

and Methodology," which consists of an enumeration of the advantages which he hopes to gain from the new concept of philosophy—solid advantages for the most part, from which philosophy will be the gainer, but all, as he states them, tinged with a very visible weariness of philosophical work.

If this is really the case, and if Croce gives up philosophy to devote himself to history and to the reform of Italian education, it is not for us to repine. It is impossible not to observe in this book (and one sees the same thing in his other books) how his philosophy improves when he turns to handle the more strictly historical problems: how such a sophism as that concerning the "positivity of history" is calmly ignored, or rather the underlying truth of it unerringly seized upon, when he comes to assign their value to the various historical periods, and how the naturalistic element in his thought purges itself away when he becomes a historian, leaving an atmosphere of pure idealism. To say that Croce is a better historian than philosopher would be a misstatement of the truth, which is rather that the idealistic philosophy at which he has always consistently aimed is unable to penetrate the naturalistic framework to which, as a philosopher, he seems to have irreparably committed himself, and is only free to develop fully when he shakes off the associations of technical philosophy and embarks on work of a different kind. The necessity for this change of occupation he is tempted to ascribe to something in the very nature of philosophy and history; but this is an illusion, itself part of the very naturalism from which he is trying to escape. The real necessity for it lies in himself alone, in his failure to purge his philosophy of its naturalistic elements.

If this is so, Croce's desertion of philosophy for history may be only an unconscious step forward in philosophy: a kind of philosophical suicide by which, casting off the abstract "philosophy of the spirit," which by now has become intolerable even to himself, he can reach the point of absolute idealism to which his successors Gentile and De Ruggiero have already carried his thought.

R. G. COLLINGWOOD.

Pembroke College,
Oxford.